# The Travelling Years

Roland T Woodward

Copyright

# Dedication

This collection is dedicated to my partner and children who bore my absence during the travelling years with unstinting patience, support and understanding.

## About The Author

Roland Woodward is a retired chartered forensic psychologist. He is dyslexic and living in the United Kingdom where he has written poetry all his life and has now found time to join other poets in his local area and to pursue publishing his poetry. Roland has previously published The Cancer Years collection of poems, which were written during his ongoing battle with prostate cancer, which was diagnosed in 2019.

This second short collection was prompted by the time spent in hotels and restaurants while working away from home. This collection, The Travelling Years, predates Roland's first collection. Roland hopes that this second poetry collection finds favor with those who have experienced the life of hotels and restaurants while working away from their loved ones.

## Acknowledgment

I want to acknowledge all the real poets of the South Leicestershire Poetry Stanza who, over the past months, have provided unstinting constructive feedback and discussion of my work. They have taught me much and tolerated this vanity poet with great kindness.

Moreover, I extend my sincerest appreciation to Peach, the editor of Writers Clique, for her exceptional skill in formatting and editing. Additionally, I would like to express my gratitude to Ann, the team lead, and Adam Smith, the project manager, for their exemplary leadership in overseeing this project.

# Table Of Contents

230 " Length Of Leg" ..................................................................................... 1

231 "For A Moment It Rippled" ................................................................... 3

270 "Wreckage Looking For Salvage" ........................................................ 5

272 **Lambs** ..................................................................................................... 7

278 **Concentration** ........................................................................................ 8

279 "Nothing To Write" ............................................................................... 10

280 **Turkey Boy** ........................................................................................... 12

282 **Christmas Too Far From The Self** ..................................................... 14

283 "I Am Just Numb" ................................................................................. 17

293 "The Duke Of Wellington" ................................................................... 19

294 " Hotels Are Full Of People" ................................................................ 21

303 "Sally" ..................................................................................................... 22

304 "It's Half Past Nine" ............................................................................. 24

305 "I Have Met A Second India" ............................................................... 25

307 "Alone Eating Italian In China Town" ................................................ 27

308 "Western Super-Mare" .......................................................................... 29

316 "What Will I Wake Up With On Friday?" ........................................... 30

317 "Friday 24th June 2016" ..................................................................... 31

322 " Premier Inn North" ............................................................................. 32

323 "Two Pints to Larger" ............................................................................... 34

329 "Yes, Here I Am" ...................................................................................... 35

330 **In The Bison** ............................................................................................ 38

331 "Tired" 40

332 **"The World Is Very Busy"** ..................................................................... 42

347 **Alien At Home** ....................................................................................... 44

# 230

Length of leg

Juxtaposed with white and black.

The gauche of youth

Wrapped in white linen

The hips unborn in black

What world are you in?

How does this fit

What moves beneath the skin

And senses life?

Starting out, first waitress

Then on to life full

Or does it wither and die

In the cold north,

The compass point inside

The being swings away

And life recedes.

Bob at the back like a weather vain

Pointing the head forward

To being accepted, courted,

Had and breed

Then long ago memories

Of how it started out,

Leggy and lithe,

Young and fresh.

How did this happen

No time at all

And now it's time to go.

1999.

Waitress in the Raven at Hassockfield

# 231

For a moment it rippled

My eyes gave way

The world shimmered

And I thought...

This is it.

Every ache, every pain

Proprioception sharp as a needle

And an icy analysis

This is caffeine,

Too much coffee.

Eat the starter

All will be well

Now the cannelloni cure

And then ice cream

If I dare.

But what do I do

If overcome by the

Coffee and mint urge,

Refuse, refuse, refuse

Done it, just ice cream.

Perhaps I won't die

Tonight is not my time

I shall sleep

Hurt wolf

Heals

Back in the cave

But alone.

04-10-99

Ravensthorpe

# 270

Wreckage looking for salvage

Not salvation, not saving

But for the pieces to be scooped up

And put to lay together somewhere.

No more bobbing about, drifting,

Loosing smaller pieces to the tide

And eroding imperceptibly.

Wreckage looking for salvage

To be welded together in an art form,

A resurrection from flotsam to winsome

A spectacle that the eyes seek out

No more the avoidant step of odium.

A new pride of public place

Not the remains of negligent speed.

Wreckage looking for salvage.

A redemption that has a fair end,

Like Lancelot, an honoured last crusade,

A mission of dragon slaying proportions,

A hand to take up the injured being

To set it in care and hospital smells,

Nurture and skill of hand perform the trick,

The Airfix kit gone right.

Wreckage looking for salvage.

Somewhere an eye sees the worth,

Sees melt and smelt to something svelte,

An inner transformation to show the world

That broken can be mended, flaws no longer,

The fault lines run smooth.

Behold a dream.

Wreckage looking for salvage.

17 December 2007

George Hotel.

# 272

## LAMBS

It's that time of year

Driving through

Going somewhere, any where

A journey that has no end

No climax only reasonableness.

How things between us tear

Never smooth, never easy,

Always a demon, irritating.

The mess to be cleared

The spillage from distress

The seepage from wounds.

How pleased I am my scars

Do not bust through my skin,

And I can feel excited by

Lambs.

7th of April 2008.

St George Hotel

# 278

## CONCENTRATION

Chili full of tomato,

no inspiration and no Orange signal,

a modern poem so addled already.

Where did Clive James find his words,

his people and his reflections?

I was robbed and this poem is a fossil,

consigned to time, a date, a context,

nothing universal in this strophe.

Must be tired and spent,

tired of tears for the want of love,

for the craving of care.

What would stem the flow?

What could be sufficient?

There is no answer only the trap,

humanity leads to fucking, and

the morning of regret.

Nothing new there, only clumsy

blundering collusion of need.

Such an illusion, such power.

Only a balance will do,

but for some that comes in tattoos.

11th August 2009

The Davenport

## 279

Nothing to write

a world to explain,

caught up in insanity

looking for what is not there.

This is a fool's errand

away from home,

lost from the self

and drifting, lazy

looking to be sacrificed,

hoping to be ejected

and then set free

to float and indulge.

No value, is that it,

or age plaguing the view.

Somewhere, somehow

wisdom deserted

and what's left struggles.

Shelf stacking frustration

of fantasy that art can save.

Sensitivity has gone,

The urge to rest and cry.

It was not meant to be like

this.

But this is it.

Now dig.

1st October 2009.

The George

# 280

## TURKEY BOY

So this is turkey land

and now no role. No job.

Thirty-four years of working, earning,

so how to support the family,

finish the job of raising children

and seeing them OK in life.

It's a strange excitement,

not personal of course, just commerce.

Ah that's the risk of being in the swim

and not the municipal pool.

A more native kind of shark,

that always swims, never sleeps,

and feeds the holders of shares

in the seas, the oceans, the depths.

So Christmas comes and Father Christmas

falls prey to Santa Claws.

A poem that slew a figure of celebration

and in its stead a profit monster.

From have to have not in one easy takeover.

I have forgotten my password already!

28th October 2009 @ The Devonport Hotel

# 282

## CHRISTMAS TOO FAR FROM THE SELF

I think I am dying.

Never felt this dead.

Slip and slide into habits,

peep over the edge and wonder

at the sense of not being wanted,

not real, not of value.

All my life I saw an end,

an end in which I love little

and on my own.

A small room in which I write,

I read, I paint, poetry of course.

Somehow I get found out and

retreat.

Wrapped up in words and thought,

kept safe and secure.

But now I take no delight,

no appetite for the world.

No rings, no chains, no inspiration.

I'm tired, exhausted of being what I am not

and too little time to be

or find myself again.

This is bad, not good, and merciless.

The dullness of myself,

the desertion of any wit

leaves me a shell,

hollow and echoing.

The reed that finally bent too far.

So,

so what do you do?

Roll over, move on?

Tough it out for all the money

you can get out of them...

I guess I grit my teeth and grope, hiding.

All I think at the

knowing I am second best to the

ones I am with, for some

it is the money,

not be poor, because it scares me.

Old and poor, my worst fear,

a life for nothing.

I need to pay attention,

but it is a luxury for those with time.

Children to see through the education

I cannot live with a fifty-year-old child,

I can't.

Everyway a bad option,

now is when inspiration is required.

Silence!

No uplifting ending.

No epithet of hope.

Not a thing.

Sane but unhappy,

too scared to move.

The end is a whimper,

defeated.

My anger has run out.

Says it all.

                                        22nd December 2009 The Davenport Hotel

# 283

I am just numb

neither hot nor cold

and caring little either way.

I am the walking dead,

a cadaver in everyone's eye.

No longer any pretense of being

or interacting in a living world.

Inside the invidious voice

that niggles on about having

done it all wrong.

Of course I did, that bit of me that needs,

to know best, to influence, to be

admired.

It has mired me,

torn me down from a delusional pedestal,

and the fall is yet to come.

The wind blows and I disperse.

This is no way to go,

but commerce like nature

disposes of the ill equipped.

No more niches.

I need my luck.

26th January 2010 George Hotel

# 293

The Duke of Wellington,

a local pub

with a local clock tick,

with locals in braces

and beer that is thick.

A fire drizzling smoke

and food rich and high.

Idle chat punctuated by bets,

giant free style spring onions,

and who won what.

Talk of sunny holidays

and sleepy drives back,

Up from southern airfields,

The local boy, not at university,

everyone else doing learning,

so where does a woman come from?

Bucolic frustration amidst,

talk of intermittent hens.

Slow conversation, slower yawns

and no direction, a meander.

Idle thoughts of "flipping" caravans,

to "turn" quick money.

Just making it, trying.

No future without a plan,

but plans full of ale fail.

So time gets locked

and this moment, tick, tick,

becomes all moments, tick, tick

and plans that get swamped

in the thinking about them.

Then out of the blue,

A haircut is needed

and locals and locality get explored.

Just back and sides, old fashioned,

and the drink,

poured, proffered and slipped down,

This is Danby.

                        8th October 2013 (In the bar of the Wellington pub in Danby.

# 294

Hotels are full of people,

not quite right.

A collection of mysteries

and enigmas hiding in service,

pretending that it's all normal.

No surprise, no anxiety

but underneath, it's tight.

Tightly wrapped people

in hard wound roles

hoping no one sees.

A jaw clenching time,

being normal and being,

just blending in but slightly out.

12th November 2013

Park Royal Hotel.

# 303

Sally

Was my waitress.

Medium rare

and coffee.

refill.

Just wondering

how it was

for them in Hull

and how it is

in Damon's.

Long the night

and slow the brain.

Typing into night

and an appetite

that lacks for

medium rare

and a refill.

3rd June 2014

Damon's the place for ribs, after my Sat Nav bought me home from Hull a strange way.

# 304

Its half past nine,

and the world has gone to bed,

off fucking I expect.

So it's me and the Armagnac,

coffee and electronic toys.

Text away the drift,

scribble the thoughts,

fill the hole;

and there we are back at sex.

Freud may have been

onto something.

Shame about the cat!!

23rd September 2014

The Crown Hotel Fashamingham

# 305

I have met a second India

and I think of scars and blood,

abandonment as I said I would not.

This India is south and with spotted tights,

and I know that I shall travel to neither.

no matter how I crave

or how outlandish my loneliness.

There is always the reality of age,

a recognition of the fallibility of the invisible.

Deep inside I always thought I might once more,

but now I know it is foolishness.

The fantasies of sharing romantic nakedness and peace.

this is not a thing that will be.

No matter the craving,

no matter the myth,

at root the damaged unlovable

like all the clients I understood so well.

No wonder I had time for them.

And now there are only stories,

and a real and present danger

of boring everyone senseless.

The blues play,

I order stuff to eat,

but at base

it's no different than a prostitute.

No one to know,

no one to hear

and save me from appearing

the self-pitying thing

that Lawrence's bird

never was,

falling dead from its perch.

The Crown Hotel, Framlingham

23rd September 2014

# 307

Alone eating Italian in China Town

remembering the cranes of Sheffield,

the abandoned shoes at roadside,

the pain of vanity was finally too much.

Those and other poems lurk.

Those mindful moments

that prompt from somewhere

something inside and connected,

that being apart, the alien

that each of us carries;

Some more than others,

the traveller in the familiar

that never arrives,

never finds

and continues bewildered.

No wonder the species

clutches at straws,

burns its fears in cages

and rages in its brutality

that this is necessary

for it to be right.

It never will be.

The Arcadian, Birmingham

09-02-015

# 308

Weston-Super-Mare wakes up

and is on edge.

People struggling and drawn,

inhabit streets with gulls,

not sure where the next line comes from,

like the addict; needing.

It's this that wanders the road,

feeds the restless looks,

the sharp awareness of predictable struggle.

It pinches the face as winter does,

and the chill is the fear of poverty.

Not quite making it,

and falling down and out.

McDonalds W-S-M 11th March 2016

# 316

What will I wake up with on Friday?

Like a bad night out

there's no taking back.

I do not feel safe,

I fear what the majority might do,

not without reason but with fear,

Their fear, my fear

what will they do?

And who will I wake up with on Friday

Will I choose those that chose me?

Or do I take the risk and trust the other,

The different, if in fact they are,

Will I be safe

and will I like who I wake up with?

Is there anything stronger than enemies

who have become friends?

Troublesome bed fellows who row like family

but stand side by side when Russia knocks.

Will I have a family when I wake up on Friday?

It seems the species cannot recognise itself

and the individual cannot hold you all in mind,

only the few, the family, the same and so

I cannot wake up with you all on Friday.

Count me in despite myself

For I cannot trust who would lead if out,

I cannot wake up with them and their exclusion.

20th June 2016 (Pre Brexit Vote)

# 317

Friday 24th June 2016

I woke up with seventeen million cunts.

25th June 2016

Brexit Result

# 322

Premier Inn North

marooned in the North.

It's inane, just mind-numbing

in the land of the fish men

and breeders.

All good people with chips,

like the food.

It's a miasma of low,

the flat land of brow,

beyond any archaeological dig.

Sucking the life out of life

nature up here is losing,

throwing in the towel.

Okay coach roach you win

I will not wait for nuclear.

So it sinks down,

no denominator low enough,

this is where the icon anti-hero

gets born, eulogized and artified.

Fucking city of culture

my arse,

twinned with Hull.

Hull

11th July 2017

# 323

Two pints of lager

and a mixed grill,

no frill, no thrill.

Trip to till

and dream until

I pop a pill,

then still.

Premier Inn Hull

31-07-2017

# 329

Yes, here I am

Clueless in Gazza

and Eyeless in Middlesbrough.

Lacking inspiration,

sucked dry by up north

with not a hope of poetry.

The grey dust of elephant people

who talk in strange tongues,

whose ebullience borders

on the edge of abuse.

A rugged, me first

I matter, in your face

loud proclamation of fear.

All the imagined hatred

of the gritty northerner

bubbling forth in a stream.

Babbling congeniality

where everything must be

dour, funny or canny.

Just a whimsy,

a pig's ear at amusing myself.

Putting off socializing

and in public with strangers.

I loathe it, which is worrying.

It's a kind of game,

A game that everyone plays

but no one knows the rules,

Or who fronts what

for what reason

and to what end.

But we play

regardless of the cost.

Maybe others are just good players,

choose not to play,

choose something else,

choose trainspotting

and an arm full of smack,

a nose of coke

and a lid for the pot of anger

that this is even an option.

My opt out?

Crap poetry

and dissolution as I read

Pablo Neruda.

The real thing is magic,

I have bent my wand

and like Sooty

become a puppet moved

by others inspiration.

Middleborough. CQC Inspection

Waiting to have dinner with the team.

12th June 2018

# 330

## IN THE BISON

I'm sitting listening in the Bison.

Failed socialist sociologist,

blagging a Chinese journalist.

They leave, clean shirt required.

Replaced by a Masters in Memory

who is a barista; due to anxiety,

failed body, big irritating voice,

prodigious pretentions and boring.

Coffee boy is with a Polish immigrant,

did psychology for a year, left,

had hypnotherapy, worked for her,

did it bollocks,

him talking bigger bollocks,

all anxiety driven.

Not stupid but fractured,

a victim by trade,

trading on other victims.

Two young women, new at Uni,

who think it's unfair that men,

fifty percent men, get on a course.

So unsomething that it deserves a bitch.

Such a nice place, the Bison.

Does this kind of nice attract

Neurotics, the anxious,

the struggling snowflakes?

I hope not; I'm here.

In the Bison coffee House York.

26th September 2018

# 331

Tired

in a dim lit hotel bar

I sit and mentally fidget

doing this and that,

with no direction,

no motivation.

I flit through ideas,

half-heartedly google info,

but decide another day.

I sit and wait.

Elsewhere there is rush,

there is frustration,

a common need unmet,

a shared frustration.

Both action and the inert

collide to produce heaviness.

like Christmas that cannot be,

where family scatter

to slowly come together later,

out of time, out of step

but making the best,

being there in the way they can.

And this is how moments are made,

the outposts of peace

where being us can be

condensed, compressed and caught.

26th November 2018

## 33²

The world is very busy

but it doesn't notice

and mostly doesn't care.

The generational patterns remain,

little learning happens,

all the while we erode,

our own glacial ignorance

wears away our survival

but we don't notice

or are overwhelmed

by the perception of it.

Too late, no science rescue

no miracle cure,

no giant imagined rabbit

out of a battered hat

to distract the crowd

or stave off the end.

We will go and leave a wreck

but one with clever ways

When you are in the jam jar

someone else needs to read the label,

until then it's more of the same.

The same gets you the same

until hope is sucked dry

and someone has to be blamed.

Bloody Albanians!!

10-11-2022

Holiday Inn York.

Printed in Great Britain
by Amazon